THAT STRANGE LOVE OF GOD DURING DEPRESSION

Michael E. Coyote

DEDICATION

This book is dedicated to God Almighty for the insight and strength giving to me to see that this work was a success to the glory of his name.

TABLE OF CONTENT

DEDICATION……………………………………...…………3

INTRODUCTION……………………………………..…7

CHAPTER ONE……………………………..………………..8

   GOD'S LOVE…………………………………………......8

CHAPTER TWO………………………………………...…..12

   THINK ABOUT EXHORTATION……....................12

CHAPTER THREE………………………...………...……14

   GOD IS SILENTLY BUILDING YOU…………..…..14

CHAPTER FOUR…………………………………….………18

   IMPERFECTION……………………………...……18

CHAPTER FIVE……………………………………...……..22

   THE HOLY SPIRIT HELPS…………………...……..22

CHAPTER SIX…………………………...…………………..28

   GOD'S LOVE DURING DEPRESSION…………......28

CHAPTER SEVEN………………………………...……..34

   SUFFOCATING IN CIRCUMSTANCES………....…34

CHAPTER EIGHT……………………………………...……40

   GOD IS NOT BLAMING YOU………………...……40

CHAPTER NINE………………………………..…...46

    DON'T LET DEPRESSION INTO YOUR
LIFE…………………………………………………46

CHAPTER TEN………………………………….…...…….52

    CHRISTIANS WALKING THROUGH
DEPRESSION TO REMEMBER………………….…….52

INTRODUCTION

Does God actually cherish you when you are discouraged and depressed? That is a reverberating YES! God is more worried about your heart and acquiescence than the amount you serve at chapel or how frequently you can share your declaration. Your administration for God is a declaration of the change He has achieved in your life as opposed to a methodology for winning His approval.

God is not done with you yet so don't give-up he (God) is at your back he loves YOU.

CHAPTER ONE

GOD'S LOVE

God has numerous approaches to definitely standing out enough to be noticed to show the amount He cherishes us. His dealings with us depend on wonderful standards. At the point when God permits us to work uninhibitedly in our lives, He might be shocked to realize how magnificent things God helps us and through us. Its discipline standards are rarely wonderful, however lead to immaculateness and harmony.

Numerous Christians, including evangelists, lyricists, and artists, have the affection for God as their number one subject. I question anybody understands what the word love implies. They use it as a sort of shroud of insidiousness - physical, mental, moral. Let individuals know that God loves them and that they feel significantly better. They leave blissful and light-hearted. The minister closes his service with this gift: God loves you and I love you as well. Presently, nothing bad can really be said about that proclamation, nor do I question the truthfulness and earnestness with which the evangelist lets individuals know that he cherishes them. Be that as it may, when Christians are genuinely enduring, accommodating God's affection with human hopelessness and suffering is troublesome. A Christian lady as of late told me: Their concern was that they didn't figure out God's adoration.

The Bible says it is a peculiar love. Observe, what love the Father has given us, that we might be called offspring of God (1 John 3:1). Notice this phrasing. The Greek potapos is a descriptive word that portrays something abnormal or peculiar. It's like coming from another land. It doesn't simply convey size, as a few present day interpretations have. At the point when our Lord reprimanded the breezes and quieted the turbulent ocean, the men said in astonishment: The breezes and what sort of man is this, that even the ocean follows him! (Matthew 8:27, added italics). They saw things they had never seen. At the point when they saw the supernatural occurrence, they thought, "This man isn't of this world." What we saw was abnormal and outsider.

In Roman5:8 we track down extra-terrestrial love at work. It is a peculiar love that a dad kills his main child for the transgressions of underhanded individuals. We don't know anything about this sort of affection. It is strange to us since it came from a different universe. It was never important for human civilization. Nobody on earth has encountered this sort of adoration. This is love we didn't cherish however God adored us and sent His Son to make compensation for our transgressions (1 John 4:10). Our minds are unceremoniously passed up that peculiar sort of affection. Whether we can appreciate it, the dumbfounding reality that God sent His unblemished Son to kick the bucket for us delinquents yet remains since it is fortunately genuine. What a presentation of friendship!

This leads us to think about God's impossible to miss love at work in His youngsters' lives genuinely. One of those parts that we typically go over makes sense of it. Each child that the Lord gets is scourged and reprimanded for those whom the Lord loves.

Dear, on the off chance that you are genuinely an offspring of God — by which I imply that you have really experienced being brought back to life — then, at that point, there is a reality that you should by and by feel.

You and I should gain and never go astray from reality that God's abnormal love reprimands us.

BLANK PAGE

CHAPTER TWO

THINK ABOUT EXHORTATION

The possibility of a caring God reprimanding His youngsters is unsatisfactory to the vast majority of us. As our youngsters grew up, we as a whole had the possibility that our folks show us love by giving us what we need and appreciate. We rushed to make the judgment call that they didn't cherish us. I comprehended that adoration spoils and solaces us, however I was unable to accommodate love with discipline and rectification.

The principal Christians to whom the letter to the Hebrews was tended to were Jews. They were the minority who accepted that Jesus Christ was the guaranteed Messiah. Her indecent Jewish siblings segregated her. The unbelieving Gentiles disdained them. They couldn't get a new line of work. Mistreatment was excruciating for her. In the event that they made the best decision by tolerating Christianity, for what reason did they languish over these things? On the off chance that God loves them, shouldn't he convey them from affliction and mistreatment? They were instructed that God cherished all delinquents and sent his Son to kick the bucket for them. They trusted the message, however presently they knew only affliction and languishing. Was that the way in which God showed his adoration for his youngsters? Obviously they had gotten the hang of nothing of God's affection.

The Holy Spirit educated the recorders to compose words that fulfilled the requirements of their souls. He started by pointing out their very own portion Old Testament compositions that had been neglected, saying, "You fail to remember the admonitions that address you like kids" (Hebrews 12). All he takes them back to the composed Word of God, the main wellspring of truth for God's youngsters. He cites the voice of God talking straightforwardly to them.

You failed to remember the exhortation to address you. A few observers have disastrously duplicated this proclamation, perusing: Did you fail to remember the advance notice? Furthermore, what grave truth did they get away? It was this peculiar part of God's affection: My child, don't trifle with the reprimand of the Lord, and be encouraged when He reproaches you. Absent mindedness is destructive. That we are so absurd to fail to remember the expression of God! Furthermore, focus on his inspirational statements that we will more often than not neglect. "Exhortation" (Greek: parakaleo) signifies "prompt" or "energize" an activity. It was the expression of caution that these Jewish adherents had neglected, not the expression of God's unrestricted agreement, not God's commitment of everlasting life. The refrain referred to by the creator is Proverbs 3:11-12. "My child, don't disdain the rectification of the Lord; don't get exhausted of it; for the Lord correcteth the one whom he cherishes, even as a dad the child in whom he enchants."

CHAPTER THREE
GOD IS SILENTLY BUILDING YOU

However long it doesn't put commitments on Christians, Bible review can be engaging, captivating, and, surprisingly, invigorating to some of them. Long lessons on God's affection are welcome the same length as the message doesn't slow down their lifestyle. They may in all likelihood always remember the expressions of God in Jeremiah 31:3 that peruses, "I have cherished you with a timeless love," or in John 3:16, "For God so adored the world that he gave his main Son, that whosoever believeth in him shouldn't die, however have never-ending life." Why in all actuality do individuals recollect a few texts that portray God's adoration yet not others? This is on the grounds that we're particular. We intentionally disregard God's outsider, peculiarly reprimanding love.

 The whole book of Deuteronomy some time. You will hear God rehashing, "Recollect" and "forget not" continually there.

In Hebrews 11, the creator focuses to the way that numerous Old Testament adherents endured. He takes his relationships from a few times of scriptural history and shows how people from various different backgrounds persevered through misfortune and difficulty. Confronted with an open door. Furthermore, the God of the Old Testament story is the very God that Christians love today.

Section 12 shows how Christians should see the hardships of life. The catchphrase in sections 5-11 is reprimand, which happens at least multiple times in different structures. The Greek word Paideia comes from Pais and implies youngster. This is a term ordinarily utilized by guardians for the purpose of bringing up their youngsters. God likewise has a method for restraining His youngsters, and every one of the manners in which God utilizes are sent as far as we're concerned. An existence without discipline is useless.

The reprimand of the Lord conveys the adoration for the Lord. "For the Lord loves him and will reprimand and scour each child he embraces" (Hebrews 12:6). Allowing a youngster to do however he sees fit not an indication of a dad's adoration. God's discipline is constantly propelled by affection. It affirms or demonstrates God's affection for us. Behind Heavenly Father's discipline is the delicate love of a parent. Here God isn't going about as an appointed authority, however as a Father for our government assistance. Indeed, even the most over the top horrendous disillusionments, the most over the top awful preliminaries, are administered by wonderful insight and sent by unadulterated love. You might imagine that this is a peculiar approach to conveying love, however we should remember that God's affection is a bizarre love, outsider and unfamiliar to the fallen. Discipline imparts God's affection paying little mind to how we feel.

The Lord's discipline is our child. At the point when you persevere through reprimand, God deals with you like a child. Is there a child whose father doesn't train him? Be that as it may, without discipline in which everybody takes part, you are a charlatan and no child (Hebrews 12:7-8). Since Hebrews is addressed to the offspring of God, discipline is really an indication of son ship. Unquestionably there were some accepting Hebrews who maintained to have confidence however were not brought back to life. They won't ever comprehend a God who does what satisfies youngsters as opposed to satisfying them. What God needs for us is higher and nobler than whatever any reasonable natural parent needs for their youngsters.

Envisioning son ship without discipline is incomprehensible. The individuals who are unrestrained and profess to be offspring of God are making misleading cases. The extraordinary holy people of the past persevered through affliction and languishing. Since they had confidence in the Lord Jesus Christ as their own Saviour, they realize that He had everlasting life (John 3:16; 5:24). Since they encountered God driving them (Romans 8:14). Since the Spirit of God demonstrated the veracity of their soul (Romans 8:15-16). Furthermore, in light of the fact that they have encountered God's reprimand in their lives. In the event that self-broadcasted Christians have no discipline, they are ill-conceived youngsters, false children. In this manner pronounces the expression of God.

BLANK PAGE

CHAPTER FOUR

IMPERFECTION

The reprimand of the Lord rectifies our deficiencies. Additionally, we have been reprimanded by our physical dads and respected them. (Hebrews 12:9). Our natural dad is known as the Corrector (Greek: paydeute,,s, and that implies punisher. Fixing implies getting back to the right state. Botches should be rectified, slenderness should be remedied. All Christians have imperfections and slip-ups that should be rectified (James 3:2). Our natural guardians have rectified us. On the off chance that it was more right than wrong to submit to their rectification, what amount could we need to comply with our Heavenly Father? At the point when we were brought back to life, we got another nature, the real essence of God, and were called partakers of the heavenly nature (2 Peter 1:4). Be that as it may, all Christians actually can possibly sin in their viewpoints, words, and activities. The transgressions we commit as Christians should be admitted and neglected. Be that as it may, when we are judged, we will be chastised by the Lord in case we be denounced with the world (1 Corinthians 11:31-32). That's what Paul says assuming Christians use insight, knowing what our identity is and what God requests from us, we won't should be chastised by the Lord. In the event that you truly understand what you truly are and judge yourself in like manner, you needn't bother with the Lord's reprimand. The Corinthian were chastised not on the grounds that they were unbelievers, but rather in light of the fact that they had a place with Christ. Cherished, let us look at and assess ourselves day to day (1 Corinthians 11:28). Allow us never to rest until all realized sins are admitted and neglected. The Lord's discipline remains calm. We are not the entirety of a similar sort. Character attributes are unique. In the event that we don't control our shortcomings, God will utilize his protective techniques for reprimand. The precept says: But he who admits it and neglects it is benevolent (Proverbs 28:13). God's discipline might be preventive as opposed to restorative.

At the point when God disciplines, He doesn't act for arbitrary reasons, however with care and worry for our government assistance and prosperity. Yet again let us recollect that the Lord's discipline is in delicate love. Furthermore, when and how He reprimands us is God's incomparable right.

The Apostle Paul was inclined to pride. It was a transgression that had not been destroyed from his life and should have been contained. He expounded on this in his second letter to the Corinthians: And thistles were given to my tissue, the courier of Satan, in case I be commended unimaginable by the flawlessness of disclosure. (2 Corinthians 12:7). To stay away from misrepresentation, note that this refrain starts and finishes with the very same sentence. (1 Timothy 6:17). Through God's reprimanding love, Paul realized this illustration so well that he had the option to compose: But we really want to temperately consider how God has provided everybody with a proportion of confidence (Romans 12:3).

At the point when you find a shortcoming in yourself, you really want to act rapidly to contain it. In the event that we disregard it and permit it to develop, the Lord will mediate and reprimand us to forestall further mischief to us and our declaration to Him. Be that as it may, we, when all is said and done, can forestall his discipline by managing this specific sin. An ounce of counteraction merits a lot of fix. Discipline is one of God's endowments. Express gratitude toward him for that?

The reprimand of the Lord purifies our transgressions. Additionally, we have been reprimanded by our physical dads and respected them. Without a doubt, they chastised us for a couple of days of their own diversion. In any case, he is for our advantage, with the goal that we might participate in his blessedness (Hebrews 12:9-10). The word interpreted sacredness is haggiasmos, and that implies purification. The thought conveyed here is detachment from God. It includes positional purification, however genuine blessing, an activity suitable to the individuals who are a good ways off. According to Paul, "For God didn't call us messy, however to be heavenly"

(1 Thessalonians 4:7) (Romans 6:22).

The product of heavenliness should be a lifestyle deserving of the relative multitude of children of God. we enter this detachment from God through confidence in Jesus Christ.

BLANK PAGE

CHAPTER FIVE

THE HOLY SPIRIT HELPS

The Holy Spirit purifies (deposes) all adherents at the place of salvation (1 Corinthians 6:11). The reason for positional purification is Christ's passing (Hebrews 10:10, 29; 13:12). Be that as it may, God's motivation in saving us by the passing of His Son is to isolate us from underhanded contemplations, words, and deeds. For it is God's will, even your purification, that you keep away from sex (1 Thessalonians 4, Corinthians: 3). we ought to all look for heavenliness genuinely and scrupulously. We gain proficiency with the expression of God as we read it, concentrate on it, and submit to it.

Then again, God intercedes and reprimands us when we disregard the quest for heavenliness. I reprimand and chasten everybody I love. Along these lines, be industrious and apologetic (Revelation 3:19). Furthermore, when he does, we should acknowledge discipline as coming from him, not to hurt us, but rather to direct us toward our most elevated and extreme great. God's discipline is to make us more astute and better Christians. I genuinely question the chance of Christians staying in partnership with God except if they arrive at otherworldly development and are liable to God's reprimand.

The sacred writings we are thinking about recommend three manners by which we can answer God's reprimand.

You can disdain me. My child, don't disdain the reprimand of the Lord (Hebrews 12:5). The word exouttheno means to disdain or disparage. We ought to never see the Lord's discipline as inconsequential or useless. Whatever is to our greatest advantage (Hebrews 12:10) ought not to be disdained. At the point when I was a minister in Detroit, a 21-year-elderly person kicked the bucket riding his cruiser on the John Lodge Expressway. His mom was a pronounced Christian, however he was mad and furious with God. She was reluctant to acknowledge the preliminaries as from her Lord. I attempted to make sense of for her that while she isn't supposed to trifle with her concerns, she shouldn't trifle with the Lord's reprimand for them all things considered. God is in charge and consistently means well and shrewd expectations to teach His youngsters. Christians endure. Extraordinary is the enduring of his equitable (Psalm 34:19). While sparkles fly upwards, individuals are normally in a difficult situation (Job 5:7). There will be affliction on the planet (John 16:33). Indeed, all who walk authentic in Christ Jesus will be mistreated (2 Timothy 3:12). We anticipate discipline in this life, however it ought to never be trifled with.

We can faint underneath. You are as yet powerless when you are reprimanded by him (Hebrews 12:5). The Greek word ekluo means to get worn out or lose heart. Christians are explorers and voyagers progressing. He's heading off to some place the objective is to adjust to the picture of our Lord Jesus Christ, who persevered through the cross and disdained shame. Christ Himself is our model. He never lost heart. Recollect him who persevered through such inconsistencies from delinquents, in case you become exhausted and powerless (Hebrews 12:3). Peruse this section when you are burnt out on life's preliminaries. We are called to pause and contemplate the enduring of Christ. Advance by discernment what he persevered while he was on this planet. As we invest energy with God's Word every day, the Holy Spirit can get things from Christ and uncover them to us. This permits us to be patient and drive forward. Furthermore, don't become weary of accomplishing something beneficial. For on the off chance that you don't black out, you will before long harvest (Galatians 6:9).

We can acknowledge it as from a caring dad. The present reprimand is excruciating and not wonderful, however it will later carry tranquil products of equity to the individuals who practice it (Hebrews 12:11). The Lord's reprimand is never without plan and reason. They are not the slightest bit ideas in retrospect on his part. At the point when God reprimands us, He maintains that something should work in us for our advantage and His magnificence. Then, at that point, there might be brilliant expectation, something great to anticipate in each demonstration of God's reprimand. Journalists later allude to it as God's. Furthermore, we should rest assured that our Father's reproducing won't ever dishearten. Some of them contain guarantees that enlighten our future with trust and expectation.

However at that point carry the tranquil products of equity to the individuals who practice them. (Jews 12:11,

Presently you don't have the foggiest idea what I'm doing but we'll find out later. (John 13:7,

You guide me in your direction, and afterward you invite me into magnificence.

At long last, give specific consideration to the way that the gift of reprimand comes to those practiced by it. We should be prepared through hardships. The Greek word gunnazo implies preparing the body or psyche towards heavenliness and exemplary nature. At the point when we acknowledge reprimand and get preparing, we discover that it is quite possibly of God's most extravagant gift.

Exercise based recuperation is troublesome and excruciating for an incapacitated spouse. It is never advantageous or agreeable to get treatment, however she perseveres through it with trust and expectation of progress. The creator of Hebrews makes this point in section five. He talks about the disappointment of adherents to concentrate on the more profound bits of insight of God's Word. These individuals stay otherworldly new-born children and in this manner youthful and untalented in managing life's problems.

It's inevitable to profoundly develop. It's anything but an encounter acquired throughout the long term like actual development. A young fellow welcomed me to his home for supper. He maintained that I should meet his significant other and six-year-old little girl. On the off chance that a young lady was 6 years of age and her mom was 30 years of age, simply realizing her age would give her a smart thought of what's in store when she met her. Be that as it may, in the domain of otherworldly experience this isn't true. An individual who has been put something aside for a considerable length of time might be more profoundly progressed than somebody who has been put something aside for a considerable length of time. In otherworldly issues, a few Christians experience issues hearing (Hebrews 5:11). They quit tuning in and rehearsing the Word perseveringly. Subsequently, they are not generally rehearsed and never again develop in a profound sense. The descriptive word utilized in this section is the Greek nothroi, meaning sluggishness or lethargy. The state comes when you lose your enthusiasm for God's promise.

A few Christians endure preliminaries, some don't. Some dislike reprimand and despise God, while others acknowledge God's rebuke and push ahead with it. The Bible doesn't expect adherents to appreciate reprimand, however it is normal to see it appropriately and answer fittingly. Tending to God's explanations behind reprimand yields advantageous outcomes. To profit from affliction, it should be persevered in the right soul. For I think the sufferings of this age are not deserving of correlation with the magnificence that is uncovered to us (Romans 8:18).

BLANK PAGE

CHAPTER SIX

GOD'S LOVE DURING DEPRESSION

BE REMINDED OF GOD'S LOVE FOR YOU

The hardest words to hear in a condition of discouragement can be "God loves you." This may be on the grounds that our contemplations let us know something else: "God has deserted me. He dismisses me. He couldn't realistically involve me for His realm purposes while I feel as such." Depression makes us feel the luxuries of our casing; however companion, there could be no other spot to go for enduring satisfaction and trust beyond the good news of Jesus Christ! The uplifting news of God is His deciding to abide among us by taking on human tissue. The everlasting Son of God has come to uncover Himself as the life and light of the world, buying for us our salvation, legitimization, and glorification through his passing and restoration; all as a result of His affection for YOU.

We can know truth and even regulate it to other people, however we can in any case neglect to immerse ourselves in it. There might be a few of us who are vigorously engaged with the congregation and frequently neglect to teach the gospel to ourselves amidst service. Work or service might be the walls we use to conceal our downturn; however now that we are restricted to our homes, it could be the ideal opportunity for us to get back to God's promise.

Concentrate on the gospel. Think deeply about it. Speak about it to your spirit, and realize that even in the profundities of discouragement, God's adoration withstands. Romans 8:31-35.

IT'S OKAY TO BE HONEST

Some of the time trustworthiness gives more noteworthy spaces of outside air. An arrival of grieving, crying, or lamenting may be what we really want in the midst of despairing. The best spot to do this is within the sight of the Lord. Distress is one of the clearest articulations of humankind, and God has given us space to deliver it. Regardless of what we say or how furious we are towards Him, His affection for us doesn't falter. In any event, when we have minimal comprehension of the motivations behind why we are discouraged; we can in any case carry our despondency and cries to God in supplication. He sees us and knows our slightness (Ps. 139; 103:14). Anything that the reason for our downturn, God is sympathetic toward our cries, for He is "close to the despondent" (Ps. 34:18).

MAKE SURE TO LAUGH

It is great to be helped to remember the things that give us pleasure and assist with easing up the state of mind. Discouragement ought not be trifled with nor criticized, however one of the more down to earth and valuable ways

God can lift an exhausted soul is through partnership. This can be achieved in your home with your family or by setting aside some margin to call or video-visit with God-celebrating companions. Nobody decides to be discouraged, however we can decide to converse with somebody about it.

Karl Barth once said that chuckling is the nearest thing we need to figuring out the finesse of God, and as Proverbs 17:22 says, "A euphoric heart is great medication." This isn't to say that we ought to involve our giggling as a cover to conceal our actual sentiments; however on the off chance that the completion of satisfaction comes from the Lord (Ps. 16:11), then, at that point, a decent chuckle will be one of the natural products! Indeed, even Jesus most likely had continuous seasons of laughing! May we partake in the great gifts of God within the sight of our families and savour the experience of the opportunity He has accommodated us through His gospel.

Ecclesiastes 2:18-26.

Does God actually cherish you when you are discouraged? That is a reverberating yes! You don't need to dive far into the Bible to see the proof of the numerous ways He cherishes us genuinely. The Word exhibits the incomprehensible length of God's affection for you. God additionally shows his affection for us by including the hard stories. We wouldn't have the option to comprehend the incalculable ways He cherishes us in the event that we were unable to connect with individuals of the Bible and the preliminaries they confronted. All things considered, the essence of our reclamation came about because of the Father settling on the toughest decision possible:

"For God so cherished the world that he gave his solitary Son, that whoever has confidence in him will not die however have everlasting life" (John 3:16).

The absolute most courageous legends of the Bible endured extensive stretches of discouragement. Take a gander at King David, who delightfully coordinates profound distress and satisfaction into the beautiful composition of Psalms. We witness David pushed beyond his limits in Psalm 6:5, "I'm exhausted from my moaning. The entire night I flood my bed with sobbing and douse my lounge chair with tears." Despite the cloak of distress David wears on his shoulders, he is exceptionally preferred, and God refers to him as "a man apparently seeking to win over his affections" in 1 Samuel 13:14.

One more illustration of a man profoundly cherished by God is Job. His life is a perfect representation that a cheerful or blissful state of mind isn't an honest sign. "Work was a man who was irreproachable and upstanding, dreaded God, and got some distance from evil" (Job 1:1). He endured on account of Satan as God permitted Job to be tried. He lost his youngsters, property, occupation, and afterward wellbeing. His companions faulted him for his predicament, and his significant other advised him to revile God and kick the bucket (Job 2:9). Occupation's persevering conditions tossed him into the profundities of discouragement (and which is all well and good).

Work wasn't bashful with his expressions of languishment — his grieving consumes as brilliant as the North Star as his broke heart drains all through the pages of 42 sections. Work reviled the day he was conceived (Job 3:1-26) however never walked out on God, realizing God was consistently, despite everything is, in charge (Job 2:9-10). God re-established Job's fortunes two-overlay and favoured the last option part of his life more than the start (Job 42:10-12).

I once heard a message on the book of Job that said languishment is an indication of critical confidence. All things considered, who are you regretting to? The thing about enthusiastically communicating your complaints as unfiltered outrage, agony, and disarray to the Lord is verification that we realize He exists and that He thinks often about our distresses in any event, when we don't figure out His arrangement. We long to feel seen and heard by the Almighty, particularly in our most obscure days, and we ought to utilize the isolation of the dull to shout out for Him. The tranquillity of the dull makes an ideal spot to hear the Lord.

BLANK PAGE

CHAPTER SEVEN

SUFFOCATING IN CIRCUMSTANCES

Like Job and King David, we frequently wind up suffocating in conditions unchangeable as far as we might be concerned. You know the sort of circumstances that make them douse your cushion with tears the entire evening or ruminating on the motivation behind your actual presence. In spite of the fact that there is a critical hole in time and a tremendous distinction in landscape and customs, the feelings of the scriptural characters stand engaging all through the ages. Whether it is bothersome conditions, lamentable hereditary qualities, or a blend of the two at the foundation of your unrelenting discouragement — this doesn't impact the greatness of God's affection for you. You don't have to take petals out of a daisy to decide if He cherishes you or not in light of your evolving state of mind. Our God doesn't change, nor does the manner in which He cherishes you (Hebrews 13:8).

I love the delightful way Autumn Miles emphasizes the way that we don't acquire God's adoration in her direct manner, "We live as though we are detestable. In any case, what you don't comprehend is that you won't ever be cherished more than you are adored at the present time. You can't accomplish other things to be more cherished. There isn't anything you can accomplish other things to be cherished more by a God who is Love. You can't procure it. You can't lose it. You never expected to acquire it since you've generally had it. You can't shake God's affection for you of all time. Why? Since God is love, the word love is exchangeable with God. Love is God. God is love."

The very character or quintessence of God is established in affection. We get the most noteworthy type of adoration, agape, uninhibitedly from the Father. As characterized by Wikipedia, agape love is "the affection for God for endlessly individual for God. It embraces a profound and significant conciliatory love that rises above and perseveres paying little mind to situation." Read that last part once more, "paying little heed to situation." Friend, nothing you experience or do can isolate you from God's adoration. Furthermore, we really want His affection to make us complete and Christ's solidarity to get the job done for our shortcomings. We should depend on God's adoration as we read in 1 John 4:15-16:

"Assuming anybody recognizes that Jesus is the Son of God, God lives in them and them in God. Thus we know and depend on the adoration God has for us. God is love. Whoever carries on with in affection lives in God, and God in them."

Paul takes us on a visit through God's never-ending love in Romans 8:31-39, and we ought to observe the overall subject that nothing can isolate us from God's everlasting and unrestricted love for however long we are accommodated to Christ:

"No, in everything we are more than vanquishers through him who cherished us. For I am persuaded that neither passing nor life, neither heavenly messengers nor evil presences, neither the present nor the future, nor any powers, neither level nor profundity, nor whatever else in all creation, will actually want to isolate us from the affection for God that is in Christ Jesus our Lord" (Romans 8:37-39).

On the off chance that you be aware at this point, you are a champion and vanquisher as a result of His affection for you. Your most profound sufferings don't demonstrate a take-off from God's adoration. He cherishes you the equivalent and consistently will (in any event, when you are discouraged.)

The Story of Elijah (1 Kings 18-19)

During Elijah's time, individuals of Israel were venerating a symbol called Baal. Elijah, a prophet of the Lord, provoked the prophets of Baal to a challenge. He tried them to see whose god could cut down fire from paradise for a penance. The prophets of Baal acknowledged Elijah's demand and approached Baal to send fire down from paradise, yet all the same nothing occurred. At the point when it was Elijah's move, he essentially supplicated and fire descended and consumed both the penance and the special stepped area.

After this, Elijah had every one of the prophets of Baal killed.

This didn't agree with individuals of Israel, explicitly Queen Jezebel. When King Ahab educated her regarding what Elijah had done, she became infuriated and sent passing dangers to Elijah. Elijah, educated regarding her arrangements, abandoned his worker and ran away from the area to conceal in the wild. At the point when he showed up, Elijah plunked down under a brush tree and requested passing. "It is sufficient now, O Lord," he said. "Remove my life, for I am no more excellent than my fathers." Exhausted, Elijah nodded off just to awaken to a heavenly messenger, who tended to him by giving food and drink. The second opportunity the heavenly messenger dropped by, Elijah rose and went to Horeb, the mount of God.

Then, at that point, Elijah came to a cavern and looked for housing and the Lord came to him and asked him, "What are you doing here?" Elijah made sense of his misfortunes for God and He tuned in. Elijah makes sense of how he was the main prophet left and individuals of Israel needed him killed also. He felt totally alone. In the wake of paying attention to Elijah, God directed him to leave the cavern since He planned to pass by him. Elijah complied and a progression of occasions occurred.

… And observe, the Lord cruised by, and an extraordinary and solid breeze tore the mountains and broke in pieces the stones before the Lord, however the Lord was not in the breeze. What's more, after the breeze a seismic tremor, however the Lord was not in the quake. Furthermore, after the seismic tremor a fire, however the Lord was not in the fire. Furthermore, after the fire a low murmur." (1 Kings 19:11b-12)

God again asks Elijah, "What are you doing here?" and Elijah answers with a similar response as in the past. This time, God answers the deterred prophet by calling him to activity and to return to work. He illuminates Elijah regarding 7,000 Israelites who have not yet shown homage to Baal. Elijah is as a matter of fact, not the only one.

Elijah's story shows that downturn isn't extraordinary to our age. Indeed, even Christians, who are enthusiastic for the Lord, get discouraged as well. Elijah was a godly man who was "doing everything right" and he was as yet dependent upon the grasp of discouragement. His story displays the genuine presence of God and how He keeps on being available even in dull circumstances. That, however God didn't reprimand Elijah for stowing away or being powerless because of his downturn. All things being equal, God was thoughtful and cherishing and sent a heavenly messenger to assist Elijah with food and water. God perceived Elijah's requirements and ensured that Elijah had what he expected to recapture his solidarity. He met Elijah where he was at

and assisted him with getting sufficient solidarity to make the
following stride in his excursion.

CHAPTER EIGHT

GOD IS NOT BLAMING YOU

Elijah's story exhibits the genuine impacts of discouragement and what it can mean for our lives. Elijah, frightened by his conditions, looked for disengagement as solace. We do exactly the same thing today with regards to our conditions. It's a characteristic human intuition to take off from whatever is frightening us. God isn't astonished when our most memorable response to torment is to take off, however He actually maintains that we should hurry to Him all things being equal.

At the point when Elijah took off God sought after him and met him where he was. It's simple today to accept that since we are supporters of Christ we are insusceptible to discouragement. Be that as it may, God perceives the genuine side effects of our downturn and figures out our sentiments. God doesn't denounce us for feeling discouraged thus we shouldn't censure one another. All things being equal, we really want to perceive the side effects so we can energize our family in Christ.

WE ARE NOT FORSAKEN

It's simple for the questioning, discouraged Christian to accept that God has neglected them. We have the honour to peruse Elijah's story looking back. We have the honour to be aware and perceive how God appeared for Elijah. According to our perspective, it's not difficult to say that Elijah didn't have anything to stress over. Be that as it may, at the time it's easy to talk about, not so easy to do. Spurgeon portrays what is happening by saying, "No one questions that Elijah was an offspring of God; no one inquiries the way that God cherished him in any event, when he sat blacking out under the juniper tree." Zack Eswine, in his book, go on with this line of reasoning by saying that, "Regardless of whether we and Elijah have 'treasured interests' under that tree of which God 'doesn't support' and Spurgeon go on by saying that, "The Lord didn't neglect Elijah and He won't spurn you."

YOU ARE NOT ALONE

So frequently we hear individuals discussing this good reason to have hope. That expression is generally utilized when somebody is going through an unpleasant time. Additionally, we utilize each other's accounts of discouragement to urge each other to drive forward. We have numerous accounts of scriptural legends, like Job, Elijah, King David, and even Jesus who have endured discouragement at different sums. Be that as it may, similar to Charles Spurgeon said, "You are not the principal offspring of God who has been discouraged or disturbed. Indeed, even among the noblest of people who at any point lived, there has been a lot of something like this … Do not, consequently, believe that you are very alone in your distress."

TRUST AND WHERE TO FIND IT

In the wake of perusing Elijah's story it is alleviating to know that even in the most obscure of conditions, the Lord met Elijah where he was and gave him solace and rest. There was no judgment for Elijah for running - just effortlessness and the fundamental love for him to continue onward. God didn't neglect Elijah in that frame of mind of need thus He doesn't spurn us by the same token. It's not difficult to feel disconnected from everybody and everything - particularly God. Be that as it may, He is as yet dependable in any event, when we are not. Hebrew 10:23 says, "Let us cling tightly the admission of our expectation without faltering, for he who guaranteed is dependable."

It's not difficult to lose all sense of direction in the tempest of discouragement however there is trust. There are numerous sites you can visit or telephone numbers you can call to connect and find help when you really want it. Song of devotion of Hope is an extraordinary site you can go to track down answers and get additional data. Eventually, we can find our expectation in the wellspring of trust, in the One who made us.

How Elijah's Story Has Helped Me

I have managed discouragement for quite a long while at this point. September 13, 2017, I sat external writing in my diary. "I'm frightened," I composed. "Furthermore, saying something panics me more than falling once again into my dark opening of discouragement. Perhaps it's because of weariness, however I battle with getting up toward the beginning of the day. I'm here at EBI for an explanation, and I realize the reason why I'm here. I realize I'm cherished by the King however for some moronic, dumb explanation I continue to believe that it's sufficiently not."

It's been a long time since I composed that in my diary. Now that I'm perched outwardly of it, I can perceive how the Lord appeared for me. I was in Bible school, effectively chasing after the Lord I actually fell into the arms of discouragement. Learning and finding out about Elijah during this time assisted me with point of view - that God was as yet present, paying little mind to how I felt.

Similarly as God had not deserted Elijah, God has not deserted me. What's more, on the off chance that He hasn't deserted me, then, at that point, He won't forsake you by the same token. We can breathe easy in light of realizing that He is consistently with us - even in dull circumstances like discouragement. Our God is continually charitable with us and loves us so profoundly. Each time I shout into my cushion inquiring, "Where are you, God?" I can breathe easy in light of realizing that He is not too far off, and some of the time I simply should be still and tune in, for He Who guaranteed is unwavering.

Discouragement for the most part should be treated with more than supplication.

Once more, discouragement is a difficult sickness. Similarly as with any sickness, somebody with discouragement ought to look for proficient clinical therapy. While God is prepared to do supernaturally recuperating mental or actual sickness, He doesn't necessarily in every case mediate in like that. He gives alternate ways of recuperating. God gave individuals' like doctors and psychological well-being experts the comprehension and abilities to help the people who are languishing.

Since persistent pressure and injury can cause physical and synthetic changes in the body and cerebrum, they can set off or deteriorate discouragement. Treatment or directing can be a significant piece of treatment for some individuals experiencing discouragement. Having the option to handle injury and think of methodologies to diminish stressors and adapt to challenges can assist individuals with recuperating from discouragement.

However there is much of the time an ecological and close to home part to discouragement, the fundamental issue is typically natural. This is one explanation two individuals might be going through something very similar or comparative circumstances and one might foster discouragement while different doesn't. Discouragement, similarly as with all things including the cerebrum, is mind boggling, and not even the most exceptional specialists completely see precisely exact thing purposes it.

CHAPTER NINE
DON'T LET DEPRESSION INTO YOUR LIFE

Specialists have tracked down numerous natural factors that reason or add to discouragement, including hereditary qualities, portions of the cerebrum not working as they ought to, issues with synapses and neurons (nerve cells), and certain ailments. Some of the time prescriptions help right or diminish these issues thus treat discouragement. Similarly as individuals with hypertension take prescription to assist their circulatory frameworks with working better, you might have to search out medicine to assist your cerebrum with working better. There is no disgrace in requiring prescription for discouragement in the event that you are a Christian.

Individuals who are discouraged are as of now managing enough without additionally being disgraced for not doing "enough."

Places of worship frequently come together for individuals going through actual sickness, bringing them dinners and showing them effortlessness. Unfortunately, psychological maladjustment is frequently met with judgment rather than sympathy and backing.

In addition to the fact that this is pointless, it's untrustworthy. Discouraged or not, your relationship with God is a higher priority than doing or serving. We see this in Jesus' collaboration with two sisters named Martha and Mary in Luke 10:38-42.

As Jesus and His supporters were coming, He came to a town where a lady named Martha opened her home to Him. She had a sister called Mary, who sat at the Lord's feet paying attention to what He said. In any case, Martha was diverted by every one of the arrangements that must be made. She came to Him and inquired, "Master, do you not really mind that my sister has passed on me to take every necessary step without help from anyone else? Advise her to help me!"

"Martha, Martha," the Lord replied, "you are stressed and resentful about numerous things, however couple of things are required — or without a doubt only one. Mary has picked what is better, and it won't be detracted from her."

God is more worried about your heart and acquiescence than the amount you serve at chapel or how frequently you can share your declaration. Your administration for God is a declaration of the change He has achieved in your life as opposed to a methodology for winning His approval.

Be that as it may, regardless of what anybody says, having a relationship with God isn't about how you can help God. He's as of now done everything through Jesus' penance on the cross, so when you have a relationship with God, you can't lose it by neglecting to do strict things.

Discouragement can make it undeniably challenging to achieve the undertakings of everyday life, including service.

You might be in a season in your life when you really want to zero in on looking for recuperating from your psychological maladjustment and let a few different responsibilities go.

Discouragement and other psychological maladjustments don't preclude individuals from administration or church jobs. Encountering discouragement can give individuals sympathy or point of view in a manner that really makes them magnificent pioneers.

Certain individuals might have to move away from specific jobs during seasons of profound discouragement, however other people who battle with wretchedness are completely adequate at serving and, surprisingly, driving in service exercises.

This is particularly evident when individuals are looking for treatment or have discouragement that is all around controlled. However discouragement, in the same way as other ailments, might be a long lasting battle, individuals frequently figure out how to adapt well to assets like directing and prescription.

Enduring is an all-inclusive encounter, so church pioneers should be exceptional to really focus on individuals who are going through difficulty. At the point when you've lived by faith in the Almighty through something as troublesome as discouragement, it empowers you to stroll with others through troublesome times.

An individual's degree of sympathy and compassion can likewise give another point of view on life that prepares them for Christian administration.

Revolutionary reliance on God is significant for enduring discouragement as well as for service and administration.

Discouragement additionally gave me everlasting point of view. Everlasting point of view is understanding that God and timeless things matter far beyond our current reality.

During seasons of discouragement, I truly relate to the book of Ecclesiastes. In it, Solomon, a ruler of Israel and child of King David, discusses the manners in which he looked for satisfaction and significance throughout everyday life. He records impermanent things like delight, information and intelligence, assets, achievement, difficult work, etc.

He pronounces every one of these desires as "good for nothing." When you experience discouragement, it's more straightforward to share Solomon's point of view since none of these things can lift you out of wretchedness. The things of God start to issue more. You hunger for the everlasting.

In any event, when things were genuinely horrendous, I realize that one day, I would be with God in paradise and I couldn't have ever to endure again. I maintain that everybody should be there with me and have the opportunity to encounter enduring, everlasting satisfaction.
Discouragement assisted me with figuring out the worth of service and of assisting individuals start a relationship with God in another manner.

Church group ought to be a protected climate for individuals to examine psychological well-being without judgment.

Unfortunately, a few Christians can be exceptionally critical about psychological maladjustment, however that is definitely not a scriptural reaction. Psychological maladjustment isn't something you ought to be caused to feel embarrassed about or dread imparting to your congregation local area.

Jesus made it clear He was not satisfied with individuals who put on an act of being exceptionally strict and moral and who passed judgment on others.

A gathering of strict pioneers called the Pharisees were the exemplification of strict individuals who carry on like they have everything in perfect order and judge other people who don't. Jesus frequently called the Pharisees out for their false reverence. Interestingly, Jesus was delicate and kind with individuals who were battling and, surprisingly, erring however who were available to God completely changing them.

The Christian group ought to never be where individuals feel they need to stow away and conceal what they are truly going through. In a certifiable Christian people group, individuals can share their battles in general and request supplication unafraid of disgrace or judgment. They can affirm about how God is dealing with whatever is occurring in their lives.

Discouragement and psychological maladjustment ought to get as kind and delicate a reaction from Christians as they do from Jesus.

CHAPTER TEN
CHRISTIANS WALKING THROUGH DEPRESSION TO REMEMBER

Discouragement is misconstrued by a larger number of people, and it frequently conveys a disgrace. Except if you've gone through discouragement, it is challenging to understand how horrendous it is. Finding recuperating is difficult, and it requires investment. Nobody has every one of the responses. Be that as it may, these are a useful things to recollect whether you are a Christian strolling through discouragement or on the other hand on the off chance that you know somebody who is.

1. You are not cut off from God.

A definitive companion we find in our torment is Jesus Himself. He sobbed for us. What's more, on the cross, He encountered detachment from God in its completion. Our Saviour understands suffering obscurity.

In any case, when you are encountering a psychological well-being emergency and feeling disconnected, it's exceptionally simple to fail to remember that God is in a real sense inside you. The Holy Spirit is the presence of God Himself, living and dynamic in the existence of each and every individual who confides in Jesus.

At the point when Jesus was going to be captured and executed, He detected the trouble among His nearest supporters. He knew the emergency they were going to go through. His answer was to uncover to them that their very reality as individual people was going to be changed in an extraordinary manner.

"I have substantially more to share with you, beyond what you can now bear. Be that as it may, when He, the Spirit of truth, comes, He will direct you into all reality. He won't talk all alone; He will talk just what He hears, and He will let you know what is on the way. He will celebrate me since it is from me that He will get what He will spread the word for you. All that has a place with the Father is mine. For that reason I said the Spirit will get from me what He will spread the word for you." John 16:12-15.

Jesus guaranteed His supporters the endowment of the Holy Spirit — God inside them — as His approach to giving harmony and direction to them the entire lives.

Assuming you have put your confidence in Jesus, that equivalent Spirit lives inside you. God in a real sense couldn't be nearer to you in anything that you are encountering.

2. You are in good company.

Look at these words from Jeremiah, Elijah and David individually:

O LORD, You misdirected me, and I permitted myself to be deceived. (Jeremiah 20:7)

"I have had enough, LORD," he said. "End my life." (1 Kings 19:4)

"O God my stone," I cry, "Why have you failed to remember me? For what reason must I meander around in despondency, mistreated by my adversaries?" (Psalm 42:9)

The Bible gives numerous instances of individuals encountering discouragement, obscurity and dissatisfaction with God. He isn't infuriated by your legitimate words. God maintains that your relationship with Him should be legitimate. His benevolence reigns even in your brokenness.

3. God's adoration and unwaveringness never rely upon you.

Discouragement makes it hard to make a portion of the "right Christian decisions" you could ordinarily.

Since I've set my confidence in Jesus and He's paid for all my transgression and brokenness on the cross, He won't ever leave me.

4. God can bring great even out of something as excruciating as discouragement.

God can deal with your questions, dissatisfactions, disappointments and most obscure minutes since He is astoundingly benevolent. He cherishes you through it all since that is essentially what His identity is.

As I was recuperating from a time of profound discouragement and nervousness, I got to sit close to a young lady who was in a mess. I tuned in. I offered my story. Tears spilled down her face as she murmured, "Me as well," over and over. I put my arm around this lady and petitioned God for the things I had required only a couple of months prior.

Eventually, God will utilize us to carry desire to other people who are harming in light of the fact that we've been where they are and come to the opposite side. Trust implies the most when it comes, staggering, out of the dull spots.

5. There is still expectation in light of the fact that your low considerations and feelings are not reality.

Quite possibly of the hardest thing about discouragement is that it removes your capacity to feel confident.

Discouragement plays stunts with your viewpoints and feelings. Numerous Christians are accustomed to having a profound encounter of their confidence, for example, feeling an "otherworldly high" on a retreat or feeling near God during a strong season of love. At the point when you're discouraged, you are most likely not going to have those close to home encounters.

Fortunately your relationship with God relies on His perpetual unwaveringness and not on your inconsistent feelings. Counter the falsehoods going through your mind with reality in the Bible.

God has said, "I won't ever bomb you. I won't ever forsake you." (Hebrews 13:5)

I'm persuaded that nothing can at any point isolate us from God's affection. Neither passing nor life, neither heavenly messengers nor evil presences, neither our feelings of trepidation for now nor our stresses over tomorrow — not even the powers of misery can isolate us from God's affection. (Romans 8:38)

6. You can track down strength by resting on local area.

It's significant to have somebody who can simply be with you and be an actual update that individuals love you.

On the off chance that you are going anyplace or even getting up appears to be incomprehensible, request that a believed companion drop by and invest energy with you.

Give that individual a key on the off chance that you are where you can't get up. On the off chance that you don't want to talk, watch a film together or pay attention to music. (Try not to genuinely deplete motion pictures and music that will take care of your negative contemplations.)

In the event that you are capable, go to where you can get backing and consolation, similar to a congregation little gathering or a family gathering. Unfortunately, some of the time those spots are not strong or empowering. On the off chance that that is the situation, it is truly essential to find basically a couple of key individuals who can stroll through your downturn with you.

On the off chance that you don't feel like you can marshal the drive to get yourself out and head off to some place all alone, request that a companion help. Have somebody who goes to a similar church stop by and get you while heading to chapel. Have a little gathering part in a similar area meet you to stroll to bunch with you.

7. Your loved ones can help you.

At the point when my downturn attempted to let me know I was separated from everyone else and disliked, there was an actual update that that was false.

On the off chance that companions send you cards or pictures, balance them in places you can see them so they can be actual tokens of individuals who love you.

Individuals frequently feel at a loss to know how they can uphold friends and family with discouragement. One thing anybody can do is supplicate. Ask loved ones to appeal to God for God to give you trust and intelligence as you look for treatment and recuperating. While petitioning heaven alone for the most part isn't sufficient to end somebody's downturn, petitioning heaven is still strong and significant. God hears and minds.

8. Looking for proficient help is OK.

Looking for help in discouragement doesn't mean you need more confidence or that you are a terrible Christian. In the Bible, we see Jesus recuperate many individuals from actual sicknesses, however Christians who comprehend the Bible well wouldn't involve that as confirmation that individuals with actual disease miss the mark on trust to be mended or are being rebuffed. At the point when Christians are genuinely unwell, they visit their primary care physician. A similar insight turns out as expected for your psychological well-being.

In the event that you believe somebody should address your downturn with regards to your confidence, some enormous places of worship have advocates on staff, and there are numerous Christian advisors accessible to help.

Christians can in any case profit from mainstream directing. Frequently, protection won't cover religious directing administrations, so mainstream advising might be all the more monetarily reasonable for you. A few Christian instructors have the choice of a sliding scale for instalment in light of pay. There is still expectation in light of the fact that your low considerations and feelings are not reality.

www.ingramcontent.com/pod-product-compliance
Lightning Source LLC
Chambersburg PA
CBHW060214260726
48658CB00005BA/2027